Understand
Reach
Expand

15 Super Effective ways to Manage your Mind

MICHAEL TABIRADE

First published in Great Britain by Michael Tabirade, 2017

ISBN-13: 978-1-9997804-0-1

Printed and bound by CreateSpace, a DBA of On-Demand Publishing, LLC

To get in contact with Michael Tabirade, visit
www.michaeltabirade.com

DISCLAIMER

Everything in this book; the articles, reviews, information products and services, is aimed at improving, developing, and enhancing the hearts and minds of an individual to achieve their desired outcomes and more. The information from this book has been gathered from psychology, self-improvement, project management based information, primary and secondary research as well as observational findings. As assured that I am that these teachings and principles have worked for me, I cannot guarantee that they will work for you but it is well-known that success and obtaining real positive change is dependent upon many factors such as your level of skill, competence, mindset, perception, dominant environments, emotional and social intelligence, as well as many other varying factors. Change is heavily dependent on you and nothing in this book can promise or guarantee change, however, I hope that you realise the change within you so that you can make the first progressive step.

ACKNOWLEDGMENTS

It is very easy to acknowledge oneself as the master and finisher of a task that is branded under your name. Although you present and own the finished product, there will always be people along the journey who are there to support your actions and endeavours, aiding your endurance to pursue your goals and ambitions to assist you in your pursuits. It all began in 1991, on the day I was born, where my parents were to embark on a journey of self-discovery and development. They entered the halls of parenthood and raised my younger sister and me with wise words. It was these wise words, solid actions, authority, and God driven direction, that fostered me into an ambitious individual who enhanced his emotional and social intelligence of the world.

Throughout my life's journey, I have had the privilege of meeting people along the way who have made a long-lasting impression and commitment to forging worthwhile relationships with me. I love you all very much, and I am ever so grateful that you are currently still in my life. Thank you.

For the encouragement, support, advice, and production of the book I would like to thank:

- My mother, Angela, who has been a firm foundation and support throughout all the days of my life. She is the lion against the evils that be, encouraging me to greater heights and serving as a constant reminder of where I am from, and where I am heading.

- My Father, Maxwell, for being a wise soul and always being the words of reason, caution, and understanding.

- My sister, Tessa, for consistently being a force of motivation and powerful inspiration. Thank you for instilling the words of God and His pure power into my heart. You have served as a reminder of who I truly am, and what I am capable of. You always know what to say.

- Stephanie, for her continuous support in all my crazy ideas and allowing me to learn the true art of following one course until successful (F.O.C.U.S). I am forever grateful for our deep and passionate love and our conversations towards materialising our visions cast out into the future. May God continue to bless you and ripen prosperous fruits for our future.

- My ambitious family and friends who have been my case studies, participants for surveys, and mentors when developing and organising my ideas.

- And finally, my accountability partners in the past and present. You are all great. You not only motivate me but also provide sound information, knowledge, and understanding aimed at improving the value in and of people's lives via our pursuits.

THIS IS DEDICATED TO MY ACKNOWLEDGEMENTS AND EVERYONE FIGHTING TO MANAGE THEIR MIND

CONTENTS

If the only tool you have is a hammer, you tend to see every
problem as a nail

— ABRAHAM H. MASLOW

Work harder on yourself than you do on your job

— JIM ROHN

Understand
Reach
Expand

PREFACE

The world is suffering. As many of us live aiming just to survive, we realise that this is not how we want to live. There is more to life than just survival. Is there not something that directs us towards our hopes and dreams? Yet hoping is not enough, dreaming is not enough, in this world we need something more tangible and robust to help relieve us from the pain of worrying, regret, fear, anxiety, depression, greed, selfishness, jealousy, and praising false idols. Due to what we sense as a lack of knowledge and understanding of the alternative options, for instance a lifestyle we aspire towards, we continue to pursue what we are doing, where the only hopes we have are embedded as dreams or on the screen.

Ironically, we are said to be in the "Information Age", yet the information we receive daily is not necessarily encouraging the true facilitation of our internal desires. Many forms of media, propagated by radio, television, and social platforms display superficiality and fear, engineered social lifestyles, and an environment of aggressive neo-capitalism. These signs signify a huge problem. We are suffering from a deep diagnosis of confusion.

Experts will try to convince you that western society's public has become narcissistic. They will point to the millennial generation (the generation projected to have the biggest population globally in the next 5 to 10 years), who is seen to be lazy and unorthodox in nature, and say that our vulnerable future is in their hands.

People are finding it even harder to find work, as companies are looking for experienced individuals for entry level jobs. This is paradoxical to the individual who has graduated and gathered some "work experience" on the way, or the single mother who needs to provide for her lone child, or for the baby boomer who has had many opportunities fail them in their life and they are trying to let the system work. The sad thing about this last statement is that the system "is" working.

As long as we live in a poorly managed capitalist society that heavily influences government, the bigger the divide will be between the rich and the poor. Experts may show an increase in the number of socio-economic classes developing, however, the income gap is ever increasing. This is not to say that there are no opportunities, it is to say that some basic assessments need to be made and executed to cater to the wider majority.

The internet was born on the 1st of January 1991 and has created an additional identity to the world, one that many delusively keep up. It has created opportunity and confusion, it is a strength and it is a weakness. Yet a device or tool of any sort is only useful if the user is too. How we conduct ourselves determines the course of our lives. Our choices are what actuates our desired outcomes and if we do not employ the right mechanisms to uphold a faculty of purpose, a capacity of self-determining achievement, and the ability to invoke a passion, then we become lost in the mess of technological-socioeconomic perplexities.

This book is the first of a series of many books to come that aims to direct your thinking and your actions towards mindset management, leading on nicely towards being the authority of your emotional, social and creative intelligence. All of this is geared up for you to take affirmative action on your passions, acquired and accustomed experiences, skills you have developed and global projects you feel a duty to deliver on.

Read this book avidly and take part in the exercises. You can read this book as an inquisitive student who wants to outdo his teacher. I am just like you, there is no difference beneath the flesh, yet we all want to achieve more of what we want. Throughout my experiences, it is very clear that your mindset defined as the established set of attitudes that one has determines the type of action that you take. This in turn will affect the quality of your execution which is dependent upon a measure of your organised efforts that output a set of results. These results affirm or reaffirm beliefs that you have and in essence, influence your mindset. If you fail to influence your mindset, you effectively fail to deliver the results your heart desires.

Whether you are a beginner on this journey of self-fulfilment, an intermediary or an expert, I want success for you, but that can only be truly achieved by you. Using intelligent design via creative methods, determination and organised efforts, you shall achieve results. Intelligently persist and focus on the end in mind. To say good luck would be an insult, rather I say "concentrate, and don't get distracted".

CHAPTER ONE

MIND CONTROL

CONTROL YOUR THOUGHTS, CONTROL YOUR DESTINY

You cannot have a positive life and a negative mind.

Joyce Meyer

LISTEN TO THE VOICE IN YOUR HEAD

The ability to rationalise and internalise our thoughts is an amazing ability that human beings have. Thought occurs every day, every second and every nanosecond, which means it is one of the most powerful tools that we have. It is powerful because of its frequency of manifestation and the potential we have in causing it to influence all our responses.

What is a thought? A thought is an occurrence of an idea or opinion that happens in one's mind; mind being the element and faculty of awareness of experiences, consciousness, feeling, perception and thoughts. Think about this though, how is a thought a thought if you don't receive a voice from your head? Have you ever thought about that?

There is a voice in our head that is consistently on, usually your own, regardless of whether it is silent or loud, it is running in the background nonetheless. What sort of things do your thoughts say to you? If you give your thoughts a name like Otis, what does Otis say to you regularly? Is Otis a chatterbox, is Otis quiet, does Otis have a lot of influence over you? Otis obviously has a significant role in your life but what is your response to Otis' comments in your mind? This response determines how one lives their life.

Listening to your voice, or Otis in this instance, allows you to understand why you do the things that you do. Being in a state of calm and stillness can enable you to listen to Otis' voice more clearly. Being in a relaxed position, such as on the edge of a bed and breathing gently can allow you to introduce the air of silence to still your body, developing a meditative state. It's not about thinking deeply because that becomes an active process. It is more about letting your mind run on autopilot for at least 10 minutes, focusing purely on what your dominant thoughts are.

Capture whatever comes into your head after the 10 minutes and write down how you felt during the process of stillness. If you are familiar with meditation, it should be easy for you to get yourself to the point of calm and stillness, listening to what Otis is saying. Repeat the exercise, but this time focus on what you are grateful for, as well as the people and objects that make you feel happy. Crystallise that feeling throughout the process and capture these thoughts. Afterwards, compare these crystallised thoughts with your original dominant thoughts.

When comparing what you have captured, decipher how similar the *active* and *passive thoughts* were; make sure you complete this short exercise. Your conscious is your active thinking and what you command your subconscious mind to do. It's like saying you are the manager of an organisation, and you have a group of very obedient workers.

Whatever you command your staff to do, they shall perform it slowly but surely. In fact, their method of understanding is only based upon simple sentences. Adjectives that describe a measure or quality of something, are not considered, however a verb is highly noted in the command! Learn to listen to your voice and write down occasionally what it says when it benefits your understanding of an experience for personal development.

TALK TO THE VOICE IN YOUR HEAD

Imagine if you could talk to Otis, I mean really talk to Otis in a way where you were having a conversation. Already you're probably thinking "This guy writing this book is a nut", and you wouldn't be half wrong! However, the point being made here is that through conversation you can seek understandings with others so why not do it with yourself?

If the voice in your head has a running commentary that is neutral, leave it to be a commentator. If the voice in your head sheds an opinion that evokes a sense of fear, why not pose a question back to it that questions the benefit of being scared? If the voice in your head becomes negative because of a situation, listen to what it has to say and either do one of the two following options:

1. Let it speak and then ask it questions that describe the benefits of the negativity.

2. Say "Shut up! I control my life!"

I prefer option 2; it's quicker and gets straight to the point. This is no exaggeration; literally tell the voice to firmly SHUT UP! If you're at home or in a private location say it out loud. There is something mystical and magical about speech. If we look more esoterically into it, it's more about consciousness and vibrational impact. When you channel the quality of emotions mixed with conscious effort and vibration, you project an accelerated command into the universe which affects your innerverse (your inner being) and alters thinking quicker. Be passionate about talking to your inner self and taking control.

MANAGE THE THOUGHTS IN YOUR HEAD

On average it is said we have about 40,000 thoughts per day, that's just over two thoughts per second! Herman Ebbinghaus a German psychologist established the *forgetting curve* after an attempt to understand memorisation. His study showed that we can forget up to 90% of information within a week. His experiments have been repeated many times and it is noted on average that we remember only about 50% of the thoughts from the previous day, which means that 20,000 thoughts are carried over; the following day we remember 30% that means 12,000 thoughts retained; at the end of the week we may forget up to 90% of information therefore leaving only 4,000 thoughts associated with the source information. That is a dramatic difference! Have you ever noticed how the remaining 10% is usually negative stuff, or things we just can't take out of our head? A question we could ask ourselves is: are we born negative?

Who knows, there will be some experts who say yes, there

will be some who say no, but I do believe we all have a "signature resonating energy field", or "contextual baseline" to which we base our level of happiness and wellbeing on. This is supported by some psychological studies where they call it the hedonic treadmill. This theory stipulates that regardless of whether our happiness levels go up or down, it will always return to its mean point. Aristotle also seemed to have found a fit for it too when describing his Aristotelian ethics which is a collection of philosophical responses to how one should best live their life.

We must be able to be familiar with our level of happiness through how we control and influence the way in which we think. The most effective way is to use the law of inception to hijack the pilot in our mind. An example of this is dedicating your first 20 minutes of the day to listening to an inspirational speaker who personally gives you value. This could be a high-profile person such as Anthony Robbins or Lesley Brown, or someone on a more local level; you must find someone who makes you feel good about being you. Do your research and listen to people on YouTube to identify with them through appearance, and begin the inception process.

The research period for searching for someone to listen to is the beginning of self-influencing your mind, because the action to look is a decision from a choice to want to control your thoughts. Once you have that person you want to listen to, buy one of their audible tracks and listen to it religiously every morning before you start your day. In addition, listen to this person on your way to work, on your way home, and before you go to sleep. Soon your thinking will mirror the thoughts resonated by the signature vibrations created through the message that your chosen speaker has incepted into your mind. This is how you control your thoughts, which could effectively change the course of your life.

CHAPTER TWO

SELF-ESTEEM

SELF-ESTEEM IS THE WINDOW TO OPPORTUNITIES

Self-esteem is made up primarily of two things: feeling lovable and feeling capable.

Jack Canfield

CONFIDENCE IS KING

Developing your self-esteem could be one of the most important things you could ever do in your life. It is a chance to really start your journey in life towards the greatness that you seek. I say this to impress upon your mind the greatness that you have within you. This power and awe has been inspired by the spirits within, that animates us and connects us to pure intelligence. This potential envelops us with a sense of being and majesty when realised. This can only be done when realised.

If you trust and were confident in your abilities to achieve the things that you aim to achieve in life, you would develop more results in your life. Even if your trust and faith were not just in what you want to achieve, but were rather in your abilities and capabilities to deal with specific situations in life, your esteem can be held high. The first steps you need to take towards growth requires confidence, and this can only be achieved with a sense of knowledge and trust.

If you revised effectively for an exam, you will display an increased level of confidence when it comes to passing the exam. This has been based on **what you have learnt**, and the **way you have learnt it**, in the **time it took you to learn** that topic. The same principles apply to you. You must be able to develop knowledge of yourself, understand how to develop knowledge of yourself, and do this in the right time before you embark on anything that tests your self-esteem or confidence levels. Learn to humbly hold your head up high, and assuredly walk with a sense of "I am who I am and I acknowledge my greatness".

LOOK BEYOND YOUR FEARS

Once you develop a sense of confidence and trust in yourself, you can overcome the fear of rejection and the fear of not being good enough for any endeavour. The best way to do this, in this instance, is to feel the fear and do it anyway. There is a sense of acknowledging your fears (the knowledge part) and internalising it to the point of awkwardness, that way you can do it anyway (how you do it), within an instance (in the time you do it). A result becomes stored in the brain where it will forever say it attempted to overcome a fear and that it has defeated it.

Confidence and trust in yourself carries your level of ability and capabilities through regardless of the situation. Allow this idea to control you during fearful situations and let Mr or Ms.

Confidence take the wheel and drive you to safety! Looking beyond the realms of fear, you must recognise that life is easier when you are confident, as confidence is a key trait we need to develop in order to prevent ourselves from developing false fears. Fear is a feeling that induces biological, organ, and metabolic responses triggered by a perceived threat or anticipated danger. False fears are perceptive due to our experiences in nature. The feeling of fear is a way for the body to alter its behaviour to preserve, protect and prevent any forms of perceived danger "harming" a person. It is important to note that fear is established through a cognitive learning process, and is not something we are born with. This allows us to see that we have the ability to condition or "unlearn" perceived fears, altering our behavioural and learnt survival responses. Acknowledge your learnt fears and focus on getting the job done for the greater good of actualising your dream.

DISCOVER YOUR PERSONAL POWER

You can draw real raw energy from having high self-esteem. Sometimes people talk about having high self-esteem as if it were a bad thing. If we look at the definition of self-esteem, the Oxford dictionary states "*Confidence in one's own worth or abilities; self-respect*". This is an amazing concept to comprehend as it states effectively that a person has genuine trust and faith in their deserved value, rating, or abilities and has deep admiration for themselves. Put simply, do you rate yourself highly and love yourself wholeheartedly?

Getting to the point of opening your eyes to your value as an existing human being makes you even more valuable and every breath you take, every blink you snap, and every word you resonate sings in accordance to the rhythm you bring to life! Dance to your beat and really respect your self-worth, recognise it through identifying with what you are able to do, and find examples of when you have done these things.

I have two main definitions for power and here they are: *power is the ability to do a certain amount of work in a given time* i.e. the more you are able to do in the short amount of time the more power you have. This includes having a sense of talent or skill that enables you to work more intelligently and effectively, or it could be because you have mastered the law of leverage! Leveraging is the ability for you to do more with less effort, gaining more time and money in the process. The second definition of power *is the ability to influence the behaviours of others*. How does self-esteem fit into all of this? If you are confident in your abilities and you know your true worth, you are respected by many as they can recognise this too. As human beings, we are drawn to people who seem to know who they are, and what they are doing with their lives; this makes them likeable and allows them to carry an air of leadership or even regality! With this in mind, you can have the ability to encourage people to take steps in their life that will give them value, all because they see something in you. That something, is your confidence.

CHAPTER THREE

SELF-IMAGE

THE MAJORITY ARE DESTROYING THEIR SELF-IMAGE

Self-image sets the boundaries of individual accomplishment.

Maxwell Maltz

PERCEPTIONS ARE NOT GOLDEN

Perceptions are the realities we hold because of what we accept to be true, regardless of whether they are true or not. We all have doubts and fears that hold us down and prevent us from really making a step over our barriers in life. We choose to accept things as they are, because we have responded to a situation before in the past and it has left a scar. This has left an impression on your brain that things will happen that way again and that you should be mindful of this. This is how experiences are created as we manifest in our minds perceptions that become truisms.

Your perceptions are your reality and it's important to understand the true impact of them in your life. For example, if your perception is that it is impossible for you to ever make money outside of your job, then that is a limiting belief that will stop you from ever achieving that goal; making it true for you; some of you disprove this limiting belief every year when people give you money for your birthday! On the other hand, if you believe you can make money from multiple streams of passive income, you will explore these avenues and try to make it work. Whatever perceptions a person held about George W. Bush in 2001 may be different to the perceptions that they have now. Whatever perceptions a person in the West holds about the Kardashians may be different to the perceptions people have in the East. Perceptions come in various forms, packages and combinations and are solely unique to an individual.

Using this, we can start to see why we have the perceptions we have. Let me explain: If you have never given yourself the chance to explore the boundaries beyond your perceptions, then you can easily say the life you live is reality. But, once you begin to experiment and play around with the realms of life, your mind is stretched and can begin to see things in a different light relative to before. Your perceptions become acknowledged as perceptions and you realise the potential limitations you have created for yourself. Take the opportunity to highlight self-limiting perceptions you can identify in your life.

REWIRE YOUR ENVIRONMENT

It is very apparent that we are a generation of "images" and "sounds", looking at animated screens and listening to dynamic music; we are, what I call: "The audio-visual society". Our brains are impressed with the constant influx of high quality pictures, graphics and artwork displayed to us on the television and online via our mobile devices. We have access to a huge library of audio files that we listen to so that we can pass time both consciously and subconsciously.

What is amazing about technology, such as watching TV, is that it is neuro-physiologically relaxing, hence why a lot of people watch it. Now, that doesn't sound too bad. However, this is an opportunity for the mind to pick up messages subliminally or prominently, which is filtered through to our subconscious mind. As you become accustomed to a programme and absorb the information that the programme is throwing back at you, dependant on your level of alertness, energy, and personal empowerment, you can go back to that show continuously for years not doing a productive thing ever!

Vibrations are one of the most powerful phenomena that occur in this universe, as it can create sound and can manipulate objects into shape. If you look at a powerful microscope you can see vibrations working at a quantum level, formulated and organised into vibrational structures. Whatever sound is projected, it is received and submitted to the brain to decode and interpret the meaning and action behind it. A constant bombardment of a cacophony that produces a consistent message will develop the brain in a way that it receives that message better i.e. if you consistently hear "vegetables are disgusting", based on your current perceptions you pick up on that message, you internalise it in a way that either accepts it or rejects it. If you have ever seen YouTube videos of liquid vibrating at various frequencies, with more illustrious and complex shapes being formed at higher frequencies, you will understand how frequency can affect matter i.e. your body's physiology. If you are consistently in an environment that states that "vegetables are disgusting", you are more likely to start accepting this statement over time and eventually your actions towards vegetables may be less positive than before. Notice what you watch and be aware of your environment as it could determine the course of your thinking, which in effect will determine the trajectory of your life.

TAKE LIFE SERIOUSLY

Life must be taken seriously. If anything let me rephrase this for you, "YOUR life must be taken seriously". Why? It is your life! It isn't anyone else's. You cannot prove anyone else's existence, to an extent not even yours, however, you feel the knowledge of knowing you are experiencing life and as the commander of your ship you have the mission in life to take it seriously and complete the mission in style. Life is to be highly valued, not boring, but valued!

There is an image that has gone around for a couple of years on social media that shows an orange kitten looking into a mirror and seeing a lion back at itself. That is how fierce you need to be. Marianne Williamson, a well-known spiritual teacher once encapsulated it best by saying:

"Our deepest fear is not that we are inadequate.

Our deepest fear is that we are powerful beyond measure.

It is our light not our darkness that most frightens us.

We ask ourselves, who am I to be brilliant, gorgeous,

talented and fabulous?

Actually, who are you not to be?

You are a child of God.

Your playing small does not serve the world.

There's nothing enlightened about shrinking so that other

people won't feel insecure around you.

We were born to make manifest the glory of

God that is within us.

It's not just in some of us; it's in everyone.

And as we let our own light shine,

we unconsciously give other people

permission to do the same.

As we are liberated from our own fear,

Our presence automatically liberates others."

What an amazingly powerful message! You need to feel the power you hold within yourself and act with it too. There is a deep intrinsic awesome power that you obtain and it is waiting to explode with magnificence. Believe in the fact that you are here for a reason and that reason is to be established by you. The ability for us to have emotion and have rational thought is an amazing concept because it gives us capabilities of balancing life in a way that is tailored towards how we want to steer it.

How you see yourself in this world is so important. You must see yourself as brilliant. You must see yourself as the One. You must see yourself as humble yet able to achieve special things in life. Look in front of the mirror right now, if you have one available, and focus in deeply on your pupils and say to yourself, with passion; **"I am magnificent, I am creative, and I am grateful for my life"**. When the ancients said things three times they wanted to invoke manifestation behind their words, so I advise you to repeat this with power three times. You need to feel what you say and mean what you say, so the best way to do this is to use your hands and your face to express how intensely you truly believe what you are saying. This may sound silly, and make you feel silly, however, when taken seriously it can shift the way you act and think about yourself. If you ever struggle with the definition of magnificence, creativity and gratitude, Google the definition as a reminder.

Les Brown says it best *"The best thing you will hear about You, is what you say to You..."* Self-image is key to looking at the man or woman in the mirror with respect, and honouring that respect by taking action towards awesomeness.

CHAPTER FOUR

AWARENESS

THE PROCESS FOR BECOMING AWARE

What is necessary to change a person is to change his awareness of himself.

Abraham Maslow

DO YOU KNOW WHO YOU ARE?

Every thought leader in the realm of leadership, entrepreneurship, and personal development always talks about getting to know yourself. But what does that even mean? Well, when we get to know someone, we spend time with them and through conversation you start to unravel things about them that you never knew before. It seems natural to do with another person but to converse with yourself may mean that you end up in a white straight jacket labelled as "This person has got problems".

The funny thing is we may find that last line amusing, however we all do have problems. But are we doing anything to resolve them? Only you can answer this and your response will allow you to understand how you operate. Do you avoid things or face challenges? A great way to start is to look back 10 to 20 years ago, and write down what you remember as your hallmark experiences, i.e distinctive positive or negative memories that you hold. You do not have to write down one experience per year, rather you can record as many hallmark experiences that strike you, even if you have multiple ones within one year. Please note, it would be advisable not to record experiences where you were less than 14 years old. Then, next to each event write down what you have learnt from these experiences in a few sentences. Next to this column also write down who was with you at that moment in time. This table you are constructing is known to me as the *Life Event Matrix* (shown in *Table 1*).

This matrix is powerful because as you write down your life events you begin to realise and reminisce on these events with a bit more meaning and thought. This is perfect because you are beginning to shape and sense themes and patterns established through your life via these prominent experiences that you have written down. It also enables you to acknowledge the people who were with you on the way, in addition, to identifying whether that person is still in your life.

Age during the Event	Hallmark Events	Learnings from the Event	Present with me during the Event
20	In my second year of University I had very little money to spend on basic amenities required for acts of daily living. A big reason for the rapid loss in money was because I sacrificed my living in order to buy a new Apple Mac laptop, as my old Advent laptop had died on me.	It taught me that I can sacrifice my money for things I really want. It also taught me that I am miserable without money, therefore I must create an environment where I have reserve money available, in addition to residual forms of income.	Tasha Malcom
21	Due to conflicting moral activities of some of my friendship groups, I made a decision to remove myself from complex and potentially toxic environments.	My friends need to have a similar moral conduct to myself in order for me to better value our friendship. I also learnt that I do not have to suffer based on the selfishness of others.	Michael Twum-Barima
22	I was promoted from an £18,000 salary to a £40,000 salary working in a more corporate and professional environment.	I have nothing to lose if I aim high in life, and that the right people can help you to achieve results beyond your expectations.	Tessa Tabirade, Stephanie Kwakwa
23	After 4 years of trying, I decided not to continue to pursue my medical career. I needed to make a decision between Life and what I believed was my "passion."	This taught me to seriously understand what I truly believe to be my calling in life, and not be afraid to STOP and start again. It also taught me not to be afraid not to people please.	Tessa Tabirade, Stephanie Kwakwa
24	After completing my work secondment and beginning a new property investment deal, I developed a cyst in my right shoulder and required surgery. All plans were halted, and my savings were used up for various other commitments; I had no money to my name. I became deeply in credit debt that was close to my annual income.	Taking financial risks is foolish without a foundation and buffer of security. It forced me to be more intelligent with my finances and business endeavours. It also helped channel my focus towards unleashing my real passion, that is, helping people to get to the next step in their life.	Tessa Tabirade, Stephanie Kwakwa, et al

Table 1 Life Event Matrix. Table showing the age, event, and learnings an individual has had, followed by person(s) who were there present at that event

Who you are now and what you are currently doing, will determine whether a person is still in your life based on who you were back then and the things you were doing. Give time to thank the person(s) who were there to support you through your times of ill and success. It may even be a good opportunity to rekindle a positive relationship that may have dwindled over time. As I am writing this I am messaging my friends and giving them thanks! Once you have completed the matrix, write down 10 learning opportunities you have picked up from your matrix, and for each one give a summary of advice you would give to your former self.

Personality types

I used to be slightly obsessed with personality types and what personality type a person is. It began when I was 16 years old where I started to become more socially intelligent and mature. Throughout the social scenarios that were constructed in my life I often wondered, "Why do people do what they do? Is it pre-installed, or is there a probabilistic nature to why people do what they do?"

I began to look at Astrology i.e. how the patterns of the stars influence our pre-determined traits based on planetary positioning, time, distance and gravitational magnetism. I also began to look at Numerology and how numbers relate to a vibrational construct that again determines the traits behind an individual's course in life. Did I believe in all of this? I don't know, I was highly curious, if anything I was more interested in why it exists, the science and history behind it and more importantly, if there is an observable pattern.

I began to analyse people and describe them head to toe based on their birthdays and names. I slowly faded away from this because I soon realised that I was almost predetermining a person and situation as well as causing it to exist before it happens, as opposed to letting life be. I soon took a deep interest into *Myer's Brigg's* and delved into personality psychology developed by Carl Jung, *The de bono 6 Thinking hats*, the four colour personality types and DISC profiling. All of this was a fascinating world and it soon made me realise we are more alike than we think, we just appropriate towards certain tendencies as opposed to the same ones.

Personality tests are great to develop a baseline personality type to say "I agree with this" or "I do not agree with this". You need data to make a comparison and judgement to get to know yourself better. Personality types are only as good as the mood you are in at that moment of time. Although, you can have the same Myer Brigg's profile throughout your life, many people can fluctuate between 2 or 3 Myer Brigg's types based on becoming more "Introverted" or more "Thinking", as an example. I would say take a professional personality test and begin to learn about yourself from what these tests reveal about you. Some of the companies that provide these tests also provide further support to help you on your journey of self-discovery. Check whether your employer's Organisational Development team have opportunities to provide you with a test. Many senior corporates take personal development and understanding themselves very seriously, maybe it is a pattern that cannot be ignored.

ESTABLISH YOUR POSITIVE TRAITS

I used to ask my friends to pick eight positive things to say about themselves, but they struggled to do so. I felt a certain way about their responses because this was far from positive

and they were struggling to even speak. The usual response was
"Erm…" then an awkward laugh. I never used to laugh along
with them, instead I would look at them with my eyes saying,
"I'm still waiting for you to respond". I would also say to them,
"take your time" and without giving them any hints or
suggestions they would slowly draw out a response. As they
gave their 7th and 8th response a smile would begin to creep up
on my face. Doing this several times and receiving similar
initial responses after a specific amount of time, revealed to me
that when you apply patience and effort of thinking to yourself,
you get answers. People don't think about themselves this way
so it may seem weird, but it is seriously a fantastic chance to
really get to know what you recognise as your positive traits.
Here's what we are going to do:

1. Write down eight traits that you think you have or
    make you the person you are – *N.B. You can use the 56
    adjectives used in the Johari Window model found on
    Wikipedia.*

2. Once complete ask 5-10 close friends and family
    members to also write down eight traits they think you
    have.

3. Place this all in a table and add a star next to the
    adjectives and/or phrases that are similar in definition.

4. Write in order the top 3 things that pop up consistently.

5. Compare this to your list of things and place a tick next
    to the ones that are the same or similar in definition.

6. Think about where you use these traits and if you
    identify them as strengths.

7. Determine whether these traits are required for a goal

you are aiming to achieve.

8. Focus on developing these top 3 traits in alignment to your goals.

9. Repeat this exercise in 3-6 months.

This exercise consolidates and confirms what you know about yourself and what you are yet to discover. The aim is to obtain validation backed up from other sources, i.e. your friends and family, being aware of the traits that other people and yourself recognise to be affiliated with you. Again, focus on concentrating your efforts on the positive attributes highlighted. If you are feeling savvy enough, you can use online platforms such as smartsurvey.com or typeform.com to compile a quick survey that allows people to choose their top three traits using free text or distinct answers e.g. the 56 adjectives.

RECORD IT

Recording your experiences and personality makeup does something to a person. If we think about the mystery behind writing things down, we realise that we are empowered with an imprint into the mind that bends us towards acknowledging what has been written down. It serves as a file on your mind's USB stick, or as a record in your mind's library, to come back to whenever you please. Let's say you periodically maintained these practices every 3 months within a year, over 5 years (20 sessions) you would have created an extensive catalogue on you. You would have produced a comprehensive collection of personal information that corresponds to traits you can confidently identify with. Over time you may even expect to see some of the same traits popping up again which tells you a lot about your dominant traits. Focus on completing the exercise above and complete them periodically over the course of the year. You'll be amazed to see what a year's worth of work can do for you in terms of understanding yourself.

CHAPTER FIVE

EXPERIENCES

YOUR EXPERIENCES WILL TELL YOU A LOT ABOUT YOUR LIFE

Good judgment comes from experience and a lot of that comes from bad judgment.

Will Rogers

YOUR EXPERIENCES DETERMINE YOUR PERCEPTIONS

One definition for the word experience is an event or occurrence that leaves an impression on someone. The question stands whether that impression is dependent upon the experience or your perceptive sensitivities to experiences? The short answer is that they are cofactors of each other. You could argue that there are particular negative experiences that happen to you regardless of who you are, leaving a deep impression on you. Furthermore, negative is defined by the measure of severity, time and response to the event or occurrence.

When we look closer at the response of how we react to experiences, we soon realise that our responses demand the control of how we perceive those experiences. However, it takes experience in and of itself as well as a strong consistent development of the mind, to get to a state of responding to experiences either positively, or with less negative impact relative to how we may have dealt with experiences before. Everything is an experience, that is essentially what life is.

Our animated bodies and spirits if you will, are experiencing through a biological-carbon based body. Even our perception is an experience itself, so we must remember that our experiences facilitate a decision in our mind that feeds the quality of our perceptions. If you are aware of this, then you can develop more control as to how you respond to your experiences to shape your perceptions tailored towards growth in areas of your life. We cannot help how we have experienced things during our impressionable early years, however during the ages of recognised independence, maturity, responsibility and the will to aim in life, you must realise the ball is in your court to be aware of how you perceive ideals in the world and decide whether it is necessary to tailor how you perceive life.

WE ALL HAVE AN INTERNAL GPS

We all have a Global Positioning System (GPS) that is installed within each and every one of us. It is made up of our experiences, rationale, practical and creative thoughts, memories, emotional states and intuition. These all manifest the quality of your system and how it can guide you towards positioning you to reach your destination in life. Imagine if one of these cog wheels within your GPS were not functioning properly, it would result in other parts being burdened by that loss and having to compensate for it. Being aware of these cog wheels and knowing how to use them as effectively as possible will position you to following the right steps towards a desired goal. This empowers a person not to be a victim of their circumstances but rather empowers a person to take control of their life and this in turn empowers a person to develop perceptive acuity. By looking back at your experiences in life you must do the following to pinpoint the source or fuel of your dominant and underlying perceptions.

1. Write down a list of your hallmark experiences.

2. Highlight the positive and negative ones.

3. Distinguish why they are in those categories.

4. Write down how you felt about those experiences.

5. Write down how you feel now about those experiences.

6. Write down advice you would give to someone who wants to overcome or implement a similar experience.

Use the Experience Perception Magnifier (EPM) as shown in Table 2 to help you discover how your experiences have shaped your perceptions based on how you felt at the time. Feel free to write extensively for each column, or as simply as shown in Table 2, but focus on understanding how you developed your perceptions from your hallmark experiences.

Hallmark Experience	Prior Feelings	Current Feelings	Advice
I failed my pre-medical examinations 5 times in a row.	Frustration	Gratitude	Don't let past failures determine your future mood. It's ok to start again from the drawing board and follow a path that is aligned to your strengths, skills, and characteristics.
My friendships dissolved due to feeling inferior and not fitting their class of attitudes and behaviours	Confusion	Joy	It will make you aware of the realities of people's perceptions and give you a better understanding as to what type of people you want in your life.
I received a big promotion from a junior administrator to a middle manager.	Excitement	Gratitude	Don't focus too much on a specific job role, rather focus on the experience and/or skills you want. Remember that you can solve the same problems as an administrator, as you can as a manager; context is what differentiates the two. Stick to a sector you are familiar or interested in and sharpen your expertise in it.
I published my first ever book!	Ecstatic	Ecstatic	Writing a book teaches you about staying focused and disciplined, especially if you want to self-publish! Have a good understanding of what you want to write about, and write as much as you can daily against a structure that is familiar for your genre. Don't stop! Check out michaeltabirade.com for more information.

Table 2 The Experience Perception Magnifier: This table is a basic illustration of how you can collect your experiences to help you change and manage your perceptions.

EXPERIENCES ARE BASED ON THE PAST NOT REALITY

The past is everything that happened before now, so what you have read five seconds ago is the past. If you read it again now, it is now, but obviously that 'now' was read in the past... confusing enough! What is being emphasised is that you must live in the moment and be present, however, let your thoughts about the past educate you about how you respond in present situations. Never, ever, let the past dictate you negatively for a long period of time.

Many people define themselves by their past, they look back at what has happened in their life and they reminisce on the negative aspects. They tell themselves that life hasn't treated them fairly and they focus too much on this "unfairness" that life supposedly presents to them. The past is gone by time and no longer existing, in other words it no longer has objective reality or being in its former current moments. What a very interesting definition for the past, to say that it has gone by time infers that whatever we think of the past becomes purely subjective and cannot be taken as fact per se. Yes, we can provide evidence to support the events or an event of the past, but it only supports as evidence and may not surpass what is being sought from the past. What you think of the past is what the past is. As the past ceases to exist, it already opens up a realm of possibility and opportunity to use what you will of your thoughts and ideas of the past. You can create control over how you respond to your subjective thoughts and ideas of the past, it is totally what you make it, because it is gone, and all you can do is imagine and use memory to create a response mechanism that serves your brain to build constructions from your past.

If you can train yourself to only let the past be a learning experience, then you will be able to free yourself from the false imaginations tailored by your mind's ability to produce what it visualises, feels and expresses as memories of the past. I am not saying that the past does not contain some negative events, I am simply saying use it as fuel to learn from your experiences and propagate growth in your life.

CHAPTER SIX

FEAR

You must control your F.E.A.R

Courage is resistance to fear, mastery of fear, not absence of fear.

Mark Twain

What is FEAR?

Zig Ziglar put it best by saying "fear stands for *False Evidence Appearing Real*." The reason why he may have said this is because it has been shown that humans are susceptibly fearful of two things by nature, the fear of falling and the fear of loud noises.

If we look at this physiologically and in terms of survival, these fears are probably embedded to warn the body that it is in a situation in which they are putting themselves at risk i.e. their chances of survival have decreased. Many other psycho-sociologically engineered fears are based on feeling uncomfortable or not knowing, and this can only be developed by thoughts triggered by experiences that left an imprint on someone's mind, in addition, to developing a standard for life.

This standard can create self-limiting beliefs about something that holds no empirical truth. Fear is a conjure of our imaginations that installs expressions of negativity. It is a heightened use of our imagination to embed a belief into us, to create avoidance of something. Imagine if the same use of this imagination was used to embed a belief of certainty to progress you towards achievement! But no, this doesn't happen often, if anything we become more focused upon achieving the goal of fear so that we can avoid the consequences of nothing. The only consequence that you are avoiding is the consequence of not taking steps towards changing habits of regression and weakness, poor results and a life of deep-rooted substance. Fear will always control you, if you accept *"False Evidence Appearing Real"*.

ACKNOWLEDGE YOUR FEARS

It doesn't matter what you are afraid of, it is important to face your fears in some way, shape or form. Some may say that you must face your fears directly while others may say you shouldn't. I say it depends on the purpose and the quality of fear that they have and whether it seriously affects their wellbeing on a regular basis. The aim is not to be fearless. The aim is to respond to fears in a way where fear does not control their ability to respond appropriately. Take time to write down your fears and think back to the earliest time in which you experienced your fear. The idea is to get to the point of really understanding why you even felt scared? Really let yourself go here and write away. Do this in a space where it is quiet and you can think about this properly for at least 10 minutes. You may also want to complete this exercise with a trusted love one for support.

Thinking about why you fear something says something about how you were and felt back then and how you are now. This is because you would have let your fear control you at some stage in your life, which means you have altered your thinking in accordance to having this fear. This means that if you can go back to when you experienced this fear and acknowledge what triggered this for you, then you could either potentially begin the healing process of overcoming the fear or respond to the fear when faced with it in a better way. Awareness is the key to controlling yourself amid adversity. If you feel you need professional help such as a counsellor, coach or cognitive behavioural therapist, please consult a professional to help you manage your fears. As this isn't a prerequisite for any guaranteed success, you may find that talking to friends, family or work colleagues may be what you need to manage your fears better.

FEAR IS YOUR SLAVE

Imagine if you were on a ship and it was about to explode in 30 seconds. Your only options are to stay on the ship and be blown up into bits, or to jump off the ship and either sink or swim. I would say the second one sounds more appealing since you have more options that could lead to survival; besides, you'll either sink well, or swim well.

If you have an opportunity, face the fear and get it over with. The biggest fear that most people have is Glossophobia per a collection of various independent statistics. Glossophobia is the fear of public speaking. Can you seriously imagine that something we do every day, consciously or not, is one of society's number one fears? Ok, I admit talking to your friend on the street compared to speaking to a crowd of 5,000 people is slightly different, however you won't die from doing it!

The joke is necrophobia, the fear of death is second to the fear of public speaking on various polls. People would rather die, than speak in public! The irony is shocking; however, this is how people feel. People would rather not have to feel or think about speaking in public. There is a book by Susan Jeffers called *Feel the fear and do it anyway* and she states that we will always be scared of things, however, we must feel the fear and embrace it to the point where we push ourselves off the edge and jump off high and hard enough to feel fear as we fall. Metaphorically, you will grow wings and you will fly through the fear rather than fall. Position yourself in life to remove all forms of retreat and set yourself to feel the fear and do it anyway.

CHAPTER SEVEN

SOCIETY

SOCIETY IS AN ORGANISATION FORMED FOR A SPECIFIC PURPOSE

You must not lose faith in humanity. Humanity is an ocean; if a few drops of the ocean are dirty, the ocean does not become dirty.

Mahatma Gandhi

GLOBAL CONTROL

Imagine if you ruled the world? Do you believe that there are people who do? Even if there were people who do rule the world, what does rule even mean and what would their aims and objectives be? Regardless, it is evident that the power is in the court of people who have the most influence and money.

If this power is used for good or for bad, it is not necessarily something we may know and can only get close to this knowledge through evidence of following the money trail. Furthermore, if you have the ability to control the economy by essentially controlling the banks, then essentially based on global incentives, you control the flow of money and you control the economics of nations. Money is merely a transfer tool used for trade to increase the choices we have for decision making, or to open opportunities not met without it.

The push of a neo-capitalist world has created competition in a way that can either be seen as healthy or ill, necessary or preventative, nonetheless it exists. It is our duty to understand how basic politics and economics works, in addition to basic mathematics, science and social sciences to assess effectively the patterns of how the world works. This will help us determine who we are and where we think we are placed in this world.

It may be obvious to some that an agenda is slowly being realised over the ages, and if so we fall victim to it every day. If this is true, collaborative efforts towards a one world unit of healthcare, government, monetary supply, media, religion, army, education could literally give the elites that be the power they need to control us, or it could be an opportunity to build and restore what has been broken; it depends what side of the glass you are looking at.

If you are interested about the psychology of how one can influence a mass of people, read the original classic *The Crowd*, by Gustave le Bon. There is also *1984*, by George Orwell, which may give you a creative insight as to what the future may hold for our society. Begin to educate yourself and expand your mind about what is and has gone on in the world. You will begin to appreciate your desires to succeed much better, as well as creating and adding value to the rest of mankind. Have an open mind to the left and right wing points of view to truly challenge your critical thinking skills and polarise your thinking towards our world. It is a propagator to act, especially if you come to the conclusion that there are agendas at play.

WE HAVE GIVEN AWAY OUR FREEDOMS

Being free is not being under the control of another. If this is the case will a person ever be free? We put ourselves in this situation when working for pennies at work, trading on average 8 hours a day for money to survive. It is also worth noting that the traditional system conditions the majority to be dependent on this form of survival and that is understandable, governments and the state need people to function their systems to allow society to work. Yet, this system that is so badly needed imposes threats to our wellbeing.

We need to be free from social stresses, free from financial burdens, free from being a prisoner of toxic foods and free from the imprisonment of fear. I guess I prefer to see it as we need to increase the frequencies and longevities of experiencing freedom, by reducing the amount of control one may dominate over us.

I've always loved to sit down and imagine and envision myself just travelling around the world and experiencing, or running a big corporation that helps millions of people across the world, or even more exciting hiking away to a private location with friends and family partying, chilling, and having a great time. I'm getting closer to that every day; freedom smells sweet.

Let me ask you a question, would you rather a mechanic-sounding alarm clock force a sound into your ears to wake you up prematurely, or would you rather the function of your body's internal body clock to ease you into a waking state? If you chose the second one, I'm begging you plan to make it happen! Think about the one thing you would do that doesn't make you feel like you are working, and go out and do that thing as successfully as you can whilst making money! This is purely about realising and establishing a system for success.

Making a living can be boring, but is usually required for survival, but you want to make sure you create wealth so that you have a sense of freedom and flexibility. Not everyone needs wealth to give them a sense of freedom, but pragmatically many people do. Work hard so you don't have to work hard!

WHAT DO YOU WANT FROM LIFE?

The reason why people are frustrated and subject themselves to giving their life away to a job is because people don't know what they actually want. What's even worse is that people are not honest with themselves when exploring their desires. Potentially, something or someone has made them think that what they previously wanted in life was silly. The trick in life is to be as innocent and as creative as child, but be a responsible action-orientated adult leader.

Make the decision today to define exactly what you expect out of life. Define exactly what it is you want and direct yourself towards it. Whether you're religious or not, belief is the one thing that carries us forward daily, so use your belief system, philosophy or rules of conduct to help you discover what it is you want from life. **The best way to solve a problem is to ask the right questions**; ask questions and be determined to find an answer for them.

People walk down the street differently when they know what they want, let me give you an example: imagine that you are hungry but you don't know what to eat, you may even get so frustrated you feel like punching someone to express your *hanger*! Your manner is different and you know exactly where you are walking to straight after work, *Wasabi* to get that *Chicken Katsu Curry Bento*. There is no way you will compromise this for anything and if there is none left you're going to the next *Wasabi* quickly! Knowing what you want gives you the incentive to act towards fulfilling your goals.

CHAPTER EIGHT

MINDSET

DEFINE YOUR MIND, DEVELOP YOUR MIND

Anyone can train to be a Gladiator. What marks you out is having the mindset of a Champion.

Manu Bennett

WE ALL HAVE ESTABLISHED SETS OF ATTITUDES

If your attitude is correct, you come correct in life. Life is based on the set of attitudes we carry. It is the way we think or feel about something that drives us to behave and act in particular ways. When we look at ourselves in this way and dissect what we think and how we feel, we begin to realise what set of established attitudes or themes of thinking and feeling we have endorsed in our lives. Life is full of many patterns and codes and once that pattern or code is unravelled or decoded, it is up to us to discard them if they are undesirable, or embed them if they are warranted.

What is interesting is that the definition of mindset

suggests that people have an "established" set of attitudes, i.e. they are set in stone. It may support the idea that people don't really change, or in essence people swim around the same sort of ideas just on different scales depending on their environment. On the contrary, some may argue that in order to think and to feel something, you are exercising change in itself so there is no way they can be established. There must be some way to break the chain and cycle of revisiting very similar patterns of thinking and feeling. This is something we shall explore in a bit more detail.

CONTINUOUSLY FEED THE RIGHT HABITS

What makes a human being become a master of their world? Simply becoming and being a master of their habits. Noticing what you do and when you do it is key for knowing where you may be going wrong. One way that people develop new habits is by observing people who they think are successful. They read numerous amounts of literature on their life and their work and try to develop the psychologies and mindset behind their actions. They unmask the patterns behind what made these people excel within their niche. Based on personal development literature, here are common habits one must aim to develop:

- o   A must win attitude.

- o   Absolute faith in your dream.

- o   Turning dreams into goals.

- o   Removing all forms of retreat.

- Taking goals seriously.

- Willingness to change for your goals.

- Networking with people more successful than you.

- Developing mastermind groups.

- Working with specialists.

- Creating leverage.

- Working damn hard.

- Working extremely smart.

- Using intuition and creativity.

- Creating systems.

- Reading and studying books.

- Studying people and industries.

- Attending seminars.

- Not being afraid to spend money developing your skills and learning something new.

- Learning to manage money well.

- Being sick of mediocre.

- Not needing approval from anyone.

- All mistakes and failures identified as key lessons.

- Using kinaesthetic, audio and visual aids to embed your

vision.

- ○ Creating mantras, habits, affirmations and rituals where necessary.

- ○ Not being afraid to take educated and calculated risk(s).

- ○ Thinking big and watertight.

- ○ Developing strategies and plans for goals.

- ○ Being very good with people using great interpersonal skills, communication skills, team skills, and emotional & social intelligence.

- ○ Adopts integrity, honesty and respect.

- ○ Develops strong and effective leadership skills.

- ○ Being a master solution finder and problem solver.

If you have all these things; congratulations! If you don't, join the rest of us. Learn to develop these mental and social habits and you will start cultivating habits of success.

COMMIT TO PERSONAL DEVELOPMENT

A while ago there used to be an African channel on *Sky TV* called *OBE* (Original Black Entertainment) and it was where my mother consumed TV shows and movies from her motherland. I must say it was highly amusing to watch, especially as it connected poor video quality, very deep and exaggerated plots, and the right sense of humour fit for our culture. However, one advert I used to always remember, said in a thick male West-African voice was, *the more you live, the more you learn.* This has stuck in my mind because it is true.

Every day we are learning and picking up new bits of information, however it doesn't necessarily mean the learning is of a high quality standard. If people want a better life they need to develop the art of active learning. The process by which one focuses their energies and efforts on a specific field and designs their learning in a way to produce desired outcomes.

People think I joke when I say this but you must commit to active learning daily. The length to which you do it daily is your prerogative, but it must be done. The subconscious mind must be fed information consistently to take it as a considered habit and without daily sustenance it fails to compute the new habit you are trying to adopt.

Make it a must to read or listen (or simultaneously) to a book that will give you some insight on a field you are trying to conquer. There is no excuse, you can use a physical book, ebook, iBook, MP3, CDs, audible, or YouTube. There are many classic mentally stimulating books you can get on download for free or even as cheap as £0.99. If you don't have a specific field you know you want to pursue right now, I would suggest that you build your mental strength and mindset first and then move towards understanding how money and society works, finally focusing on a desired skill you want to develop. Top it off by booking yourself on free workshops and seminars, meeting new people and test the waters in order to increase possibility of opportunity.

Jim Rohn once said *"we get paid for bringing value to the market place,"* you will understand what that means throughout the rest of the book.

CHAPTER NINE

MAKING THE SHIFT

COMMITMENT TO CHANGE IS WHAT CREATES CHANGE

Change your thoughts and you change your world.

Norman Vincent Peale

CHANGE ARRIVES FOR SERIOUS PEOPLE

We have established part of who you are at the beginning of this book by looking at what experiences have shaped you as a person, which are also based on the thoughts you produce, and actions associated with those thoughts. We develop habits that shape the persona that people place on us. Whatever you focus your energy on is what you are serious about; as I once said to one of my coaching clients *"we are what we prioritise"*.

Let's say you are in an argument and you focus your energy on continuously arguing about who is right, that is what you are serious about in that moment of time; if you focus your energy 6 days a week on sprint training in preparation for the next Olympics, that's what you are serious about; if you focus

11 hours of your day working at a hospital, that is what you are serious about. Excuses and reasons mean nothing, because what you do is what tells. Being serious about an event or activity doesn't mean you necessarily want to do it, but because of avoidance of some form of pain you invest a lot of your time doing it.

Being creatures of reason we like to use our reasoning when we feel necessary, but if a group of extraterrestrial beings were to watch you and observe your daily habits without context behind them, they may become perplexed by your repetitive activities. Even if you were to have what seemed to be valid reasons for your actions, these reasons may never had crossed their minds. If you have something that you would like to do in your life, think about how serious you are about doing it. The repetitiveness of one's actions displays a quality of seriousness towards a desired goal. If you're not working towards your goals, then that indicates a lack of seriousness towards them, if you're making moves towards attaining them, then you're showing a level of seriousness and respect for your goals, and if you're doing what you set out to achieve, then no one can say you're not doing it. Learn to watch yourself from inside-out, and remove any form of reason behind supporting the 'lack of' doing something you desire.

YOUR ENVIRONMENT DETERMINES THE QUALITY OF YOUR RESULTS

There are many forms of environment around us and if we look at the definition of environment, we realise that it is *the surroundings or conditions in which a person operates*. From this definition we can deduce that our environment is pretty much everything that affects us as a person, from our genetics, to the food we eat, to even the continuous use of our mobile phone to our preferred ear.

Think about it, imagine if you had the supreme power and drive to truly transform your conditions and surroundings, better yet change the way you operate! You do have that power it was given to you! It is about realising how much your environment does influence you and how you can change it at will. For example, if you are constantly surrounded by chocolates and biscuits and like to eat out for lunch, imagine 6 weeks later you realise your waist has gone 6 inches thicker, it's not hard to soon realise that your environment contributed towards your new waistline. However, your response in that environment was the overall determinant behind why you went from a medium waist to a large waist. All your environment does is increase the chance of something occurring based on the conditioning of your response to that environment. It does not mean that your environment defines your actions, all it means is that based on patterns of behaviour, history and observation reveals that you may respond a particular way.

You may not necessarily have to have had that exact same experience; remember habits are transferrable and your mindset shapes a lot of what you do. Be mindful of your environment and learn how to respond to it appropriately.

YOU ARE AN INTRICATE PRODUCT OF YOUR NETWORK

I'm sure you've heard the saying your network is your net worth. Many entrepreneurs and leaders in industry use this term because they have seen that networking creates opportunity. There is a saying in sales that says you must go through the numbers before you find the right prospect, have you ever applied this to your life? There are people who are in our life for a season and people who are in our life for a reason. Reasons change and people appear to as well.

It is in your own invested interest to be nice, sociable and an effective communicator for the sake of it. Life shows us that with the law of averages you are bound to find someone who will serve as a great reason for their existence in your life. The law of averages will also state that someone based on the law of reciprocity (indirect or direct), will respond to your "nice-attitude" favourably. Even more than anything, decide what you want in life and then hang around areas offline and online that associate you with like-minded people. The feeling of talking to someone who is on your wavelength is such a refreshing feeling. Aim to experience that feeling as much as possible. Subscribe to people and events that will increase your network! For those of you who are looking to increase their network and develop a skill, or just to meet new people check out these sites, platforms and applications for events.

- Meetup

- Eventbrite

- Excel centre

- O2 Arena

- Network marketing companies

- Property networks and workshops

- Toastmasters International

- Edward de Bono Conversation Clubs

- Online marketing workshops

- Book clubs

- Library clubs

- Exercise groups and sports clubs

- Travel groups

- Food and wine tasting groups

- Cooking groups

- Personal development seminars

This is not an exhaustive list however, it is a place to start. Better yet, the top four on this list are likely to encapsulate all the groups and clubs below them. You may have many interests but invest your time in just 1 or 2, it is much easier to manage and once you get used to fitting it into your schedule you can go to another.

Attend a networking event at least 3 times and if it is not for you move on, but the aim is to network and make an effort towards meeting new people and finding out about their lives – it is not about you. Don't think of it as networking, rather see it as having a conversation amongst people who have the potential to be your great friends in the future, and engage with them in a way where you understand their motivations in life.

"A superior man is modest in his speech, but exceeds in his actions" –
Confucius.

CHAPTER TEN

WILLPOWER

WILLPOWER IS NEVER ENOUGH

I believe in one thing only, the power of human will.

Joseph Stalin

EMOTIONS RUN THE SHOW

The will for a person to do something is essentially a decision a person makes on their own. When willpower is employed towards a specific action (or not) it is deliberate. If a person attends a motivational event and hears the words from the speaker "No one is going to write your book for you but you", that may activate the "willpower button" in a person for them to say "I am going to use all my willpower to write this book!". They go home and start writing.

A week later they've stopped. Was their original statement a lie? No, it wasn't, they did use all their will to start writing their book. Yet they did not persevere and in result did not have a complete book. The problem is it wasn't a real decision. They didn't plan for success, they let emotional hype carry them on a journey, rather than channelling that emotion into a bullet proof "retreatless" solution. **Willpower is real power when followed through to completion,** when you have a burning desire to succeed regardless of motivation, and when you position yourself to achieve the heights of your goals.

The willpower you exercise is dependent upon the source that ignites your emotional centres to enable one to take action.

WILLPOWER IS NOT STICKY

Now that we have established willpower we can be sure to understand the difference between saying you are going to do something based on a motivational influence, or saying you are going to do it based on your planning and smart yet hard grafting. Do not trust anyone, including yourself, who says they are going to do something the day they have been exposed to motivation. There is a statistic that shows that 85% of people fail to complete their new year's resolutions 15 days after they make them. It goes to show it is cultural and somewhat feels intuitive to want to show people, and yourself, that you are special and that you do not fit the similar patterns as the rest of the human species.

If we look at what special means it is defined as *different to what is usual,* so why do people do what is usual when making a "new commitment"? It's because they don't know what commitment requires and it shows in their language when referring to the use of willpower. Break the pattern, break the mould and observe how the unusual truly use willpower and stick to their commitments.

COMMITMENT ALWAYS WINS

Imagine if a vet stopped operating on a cat during surgery because she couldn't be bothered anymore and left them under anaesthetic open and bare? Do you think that it is fair on the cat and its owner(s)? Doesn't sound like it. Even if the vet didn't want to perform surgery anymore she is legally bound and has a duty of care based on integrity and fulfilment to be responsible to follow through on her word.

Commitment is doing the thing you said you were going to do long after the feeling has gone and persistently until completion. Sounds painful, doesn't it? Think about all the things you once said you were going to do, but you never actually did. Imagine if you followed through, where would your life be now? Let's not lie about the fact that commitment is a strong tool, however it is too boring and long for many people to endure. If you agree that the dynamics of love change in the beginning of your first 3 months in a relationship, compared to the next 30 years in a relationship, then you'll understand the key part that commitment plays and pays.

With clear sight of your vision in mind commitment can be played well, because you are passionately set on achieving your end desired goal. If there is no desire attached to the vision, it's delusion. So, in order for you to be truly committed, there must be some bait at the end of the line that you are crazy enough to chase... Forever.

CHAPTER ELEVEN

DETERMINATION

DETERMINATION CLOSES THE GAP BETWEEN NOW AND YOUR GOALS

Failure will never overtake me if my determination to succeed is strong enough.

Og Mandino

ENTHUSIASM IS THE COUSIN OF DETERMINATION

I admire those individuals who transform into beast mode with their ambitions! They are inspiring to watch, they almost remind me of a lioness chasing a gazelle from far, knowing it is going to hunt it down and feast like a Queen by the end of the night. Imagine that ferocious, roaring and all-demanding muscle, chasing you down to the point where you feel you don't have any choice but to be the lunch. There is a firmness of purpose mixed with an intense and eager desire to achieve their task... Eat.

I want you also to imagine being extremely hungry after a 10-hour day at work. In your mind, you have been visualising exactly what you want to eat, you want a traditional West-African dish known as Jollof Rice, dressed with a light tomato based sauce, surrounded by fried plantain, fried chicken, and coleslaw. You almost run home to devour this meal, anything that gets in your way does not stop you from what you want, because you know exactly what you want. You finally race to your door, open it wide, go to the kitchen and watch a family member break the last chicken wing that was supposed to go in your mouth. Love turns to hate quickly. However, you are determined and you prepare the meal yourself. 90 minutes later, you sit back, listen to some chilled music, and eat your dinner in passionate peace.

You were determined, but energy and enthusiasm carried you through! When you do things with positive intense energy with a goal in mind, that is determination. No one, absolutely no one, can stop you. Even if life wants to test you, you've decided you're winning, and it's non-negotiable. Be enthusiastic in life, do what you love and love what you do because that is the antidote to living a successful life.

YOU NEED A "NO MATTER WHAT" ATTITUDE

We've already highlighted above that when we want something so bad, we are willing to go the extra mile. Why do we do that? It's like a split second intense madness that snaps inside your mind and releases a bundling ball of fire, blazing inside you creating that desire to want to win and not give up, regardless of your conditions or circumstances. We decide that we are not settling for anything less than the best! With this mindset you don't fear death, because death in this instance is the only thing that can stop you. Start to see what this sort of attitude can do for you; begin to absorb the sorts of results you could produce; and truly grasp how it makes you stand out from the crowd.

I really admire long distance runners; people forget they weren't always at the level they are at now. But at some point, in their life they decided they weren't going to stop running, they wanted to run until life stopped them. The sheer determination and enthusiasm it must take to drive yourself through the physical pain and barriers of restricted breathing is beyond me. If you want to understand what a "no matter what" attitude is, study athletes and watch how they train, live and act all year round and compare that to their performance. If you can do what they do i.e. train in adverse weather conditions, eat the right food when you don't want too, and wake up at ungodly times of the day to train, then you have a "no matter what" it takes attitude. If you prefer excuses, then it may take you time to set yourself apart from the crowd and get closer to your goals. Learn to cut all excuses, respond to them well, and do whatever it takes (with integrity) to excel in life.

DETERMINATION GETS YOU RESULTS

Results never lie. Results give you an answer. That's what life's about, finding information that formulates an answer that gives you choices to decide. Results are important to embed a belief in your mind, it creates a personal certainty that you are accustomed too. If you want your life to change, focus on obtaining results and measuring and monitoring your results to start moulding them into results that you want. That's how the game works.   Focus on your strengths and develop them because they are your strengths for a reason; they have proven to get you results. Yes, it is important to be competent even with your weaknesses, however, do not waste time developing something when life has proven that you are disadvantaged against developing yourself in that given area.

Every great individual starts off with a theory or a question that they want answered. As an example, it could be the idea that someone believes that they have the skills to be an effective motivational speaker, and want to inspire people who need direction in their lives. Here is what someone like that might do: Research is conducted to gain better insights behind case studies of successful and unsuccessful public speakers, the industry as a whole, how the business is setup, as well as many other factors. A hypothesis is formulated and may read "it is possible for me to be a public speaker, and make a living from it". In order to confirm or disprove this hypothesis, a test, method or plan of action is tried in order to conduct an experiment carefully, including what can be done to make sure the results are successful according to the hypothesis. Once the method has been tried the results are analysed to see whether the method of execution was appropriate. In addition, the observations may be reviewed to find areas for improvement. Analysis and reviews can be done once the results are recorded in a pragmatic fashion. Results may be discussed with an objective person to validate whether the hypothesis was accurate or not. I dare you to follow this structure to discover if you could achieve your goals!

In *Table 3* the *Scientific Achievement Model* or SAM for short, is modelled after the traditional scientific method. It establishes a robust way of executing your plans in a logical manner. Use this scientific model to plan and capture your success.

The Traditional Scientific Method	The Scientific Achievement Model (SAM)
Questioning a topic or problem.	Challenging the status quo and defining your strengths, skills, passion and purpose.
Conduct academic research.	Consolidating understanding by identifying where you fit in the word through primary and secondary research (consciously or sub-consciously).
Construct a hypothesis.	Establishing self-belief through faith as well as developing affirmations.
Employ a method.	Developing Goals, Objectives and an Action Plan. Strategically plan your positioning in an environment that fosters success.
Analyse results.	Regularly implement critical examination and feedback on your experiences, actions and results, discovering what works and what doesn't work.
Discussion based around the observations.	Reflect and review your plan, make iterations where necessary and discuss with other people who are aligned to your desired goals.

Table 3 The Traditional Scientific Method Vs The Scientific Achievement Model (SAM)

CHAPTER TWELVE

IMAGINATION

IMAGINATION IS THE POWER BEHIND EVERYTHING

What is now proved was once only imagined.

William Blake

EVERYTHING IS THE RESULT OF IMAGINATION

Look around you, everything in your sight was created either directly or indirectly from people, or by nature. But ultimately didn't it all begin with creative and expressive thought? Even Mother Nature appears to use a rhythm that creates into existence. As human beings, we use the artistic form of imagination to not only visualise what we want, but also to invoke a feeling. "Visualisation" + "Directed Emotion" creates an energetic driving force that allows fruit to grow, become ripe and be plucked for the harvest.

People today suffer from a lack of imagination, they suffer from a severe complex of being able to dream about things and execute them into the realm of the living. This is partly because technology has substituted the imaginative and creative faculties within our minds by what we are conditionally exposed to frequently on media platforms and the internet. People do not realise that everything around them is a result of the few that took their imaginations extremely seriously, so serious that they made it tangibly known to the world in some shape or form; a testimony of this is this very book that you are reading.

If you continue to restrict your imaginative flow, you are preventing someone else from receiving value through you. There is someone waiting for you to deliver your product, service, or idea, but because you lack the capacity to imagine, dream and follow through, they will get nothing and potentially continue to suffer. You may not care as you may not know the person(s), but on the contrary, think about the things you need to feed your feelings of happiness in the materialistic, spiritual and financial realm. Think about ways in which you can initiate your imaginative juices, and excite your life with colour!

TURN THE INVISIBLE INTO THE VISIBLE

Thought is a powerful resource as it is a combination of opinions and ideas that appear in the mind, influenced by our consciousness and emotional states, as well as our environment. This statement also highlights that emotions can bring about a direction of thought and can even push you to exercise the ideas that appear in your mind. So, controlled thought, coupled with funnelled emotion, can harbour a result of turning things from the invisible to the visible.

All things existent on earth are not necessarily perceptive to our senses. Therefore, one may deduce that things came to be from a state of nothingness (or things we cannot see and feel), but was attached to a string of thought, intelligent energy, consciousness, or even an organised vibrational mechanistic system. Reducing from a universal to a human level, this infers that with the right sort of thoughts and emotion you can create! We are all creators and inventors ladies and gentlemen, some of us have not realised it yet due to the disinformation fed into our minds.

We were born to make, write, speak, sing and serve our fellow brothers and sisters. Dare to dream and act on the invisible that lies dormant in your head.

There is a saying by Myles Munroe that says:

"The wealthiest places in the world are not gold mines, oil fields, diamond mines or banks. The wealthiest place is the cemetery. There lies companies that were never started, masterpieces that were never painted... In the cemetery, there is buried the greatest treasure of untapped potential. There is a treasure within you that must come out. Don't go to the grave with your treasure still within YOU."

What a way to slap you in the face, wake up and stop thinking you're not good enough! Go back and start this book again if you still think you're not worthy enough to start on your ambitions. There is no point reading this book for leisure if you are not willing to be different, jump out of your comfort zone, try something new and make things happen.

GO AS WILD AS YOU WANT AND REALISE YOUR DREAM

Google's definition of "crazy" is *mad, especially as manifested in wild or aggressive behaviour or extremely enthusiastic.* I think this is fitting for the realisation and actualisations of dreams. The more emotionally charged you are towards it, the bigger and bolder you will be when performing the exercises towards it. This is the beauty of deciding to follow your true passions, priorities, desires, and problems you want to solve. It allows you to go as big and as bold as you want, or as small and as discrete as you want, it's totally in your hands.

If money wasn't an object and at will you could create your dream right now, think about what you would do. Keeping this in mind, what would you need to do in order to start actualising your dream as soon as possible? Now, *Just Do it!* That is what going crazy and wild is. Do not be set back by people who continuously say you are insane, or you can't do something. Let their comments prove them wrong. Every highly successful and influential person is crazy, because they:

1. Believed they could do something different.

2. Believed they were The One.

3. Never responded regressively to people's negative opinions.

Your dream should make you smile like a little kid. If you are a visual person create a vision board and see how many times the corners of your lips rise ever closer to your eyes. Be brave to dream intensely and start making plans to exude it into being.

CHAPTER THIRTEEN

BEHAVIOUR CHANGE

DEVELOP THE DISCIPLINE TO TAKE AFFIRMATIVE ACTION

What is now proved was once only imagined.

William Blake

POSITION YOURSELF FOR SUCCESS

Coordinate yourself on the chessboard so that you have a better chance of attacking the King. In other words remove everything that makes you feel comfortable, or increases your chances of proclaiming never-ending excuses. The aim is to make your next move regardless of your situations. Make the right first steps by disassembling any forms of escape.

All successful leaders experience and feel emotions associated with fear, however they do not respond to it like everyone else; they *Feel the fear, and do it anyway.* The best way to do this is to take in the feeling of fear and in that moment act on it with impulse. If the impulsive moment has gone, you need to create strategies to position yourself again. Get someone to coach you or get you to perform a task in a specific timeframe to drive a result. Get this person to continually do this until you get the result you need.

In the book *Talk like TED* by Carmine Gallo, it reads that every time you perform an activity continuously, an area in the brain changes in shape or size as a neurophysiological response to that activity. Darren Hardy, CEO of *Success Magazine* states that it takes about 300 continuous attempts of an act before an impressionable groove in the brain is conspicuous.

The best way to develop this is by *behavioural strategic positioning*. This is setting up your environment to encourage positive and desired behaviours for a desired outcome, with the aim to overcome prior incongruent habits. Strategic thinking and environmental setup is paramount for success. Some people leave their wallets at home to stop them from spending unnecessarily, others buy nuts and fruits at work to stop them from eating cakes and crisps, other people may even setup a monthly direct debit that goes into an account that can't be accessed for 5 years to save money. It's about thinking creatively, and outthinking yourself, so that you know rain or shine you must do what you positioned yourself to do. **Position yourself in life, and life will position you.**

PROCLAIM YOUR GOALS TO THE WORLD

Have you ever noticed that people go through a stage of not telling people anything about their lives, and then they go through a period where they say everything, and then it swaps again? It's because people do not behave according to a standard. They want to do things undercover and eventually surprise people to the point where they are like "Oh my days, when did that happen?!?" Why do we want to surprise people so much? It's a little strange because when you have accomplished your goal, the excited feeling dies down after a while. Don't get me wrong the behaviour produces a great feeling if you've successfully achieved a goal, and it is understandable why people do it, especially if people doubted them in the past, but sometimes your strategy needs to be different.

One way to position yourself for success, especially long after the feeling has gone, is to publicly explain what it is you set out to do and how long you plan to do it for. The thought of it makes some people want to get swallowed up by the ground. However, for the people who understand this psychology, this is a great tactic and works well if developed properly. It doesn't necessarily mean post it on Facebook, however it can mean bring it up in real human face-to-face conversations.

The idea is to first plan exactly what you set out to do and put everything in place to do it. The preparation stage is key because it develops the confidence needed to get you started. Do not stay in this phase for too long otherwise you may chicken yourself out of it. Once you are ready, begin making it a natural topic of conversation.

If you do have a following or are comfortable with social media, then of course you can produce a social media post with maybe a picture, geotag, and/or tag of some friends to grab some attention! A daily or weekly blog or vlog is another way to create accountability. Be creative about the process and be ready to perform on stage to win your prize! If you do not successfully achieve what you want to achieve, at least you tried it and you have it on record. It is so much better than just thinking about doing it. This in essence, will give you the strength to even try again, learn from your lessons and deem yourself successful.

BUILD YOUR VISION

Vision is key to any endeavour. If you fail to have vision stop everything you are doing and get vision… Please take me very seriously because vision fuels the emotional and determination tank needed to drive your burning desire to succeed. Vision uses the supreme faculties of imagination that are intertwined with the wisdom you have enveloped within a specific field. Les Brown puts it so deliciously as he said *"people say if you see it you believe it, I say if you believe it you can see it."* He is completely right. If you do not agree, I'm sorry. Nonetheless, here is how you create a vision:

Step 1: Decide what you want: Sit down and write a list of all the things you want and then next to them write down why you want it. In addition, next to that think about and write down how it would make you feel if you were to get that thing.

Step 2: Review your life: Go back to your life event matrix and think about what you have learnt in life. Think about where Life has taken you and write a paragraph or so that expresses where you are at now.

Step 3: Make your vision feel real: Go back to step 1 and gather props or pictures (if digital you can use Pinterest or Google Keep) to create a vision board of your desires. You can also create a separate vision board of inspiring thought leaders in your desired field who have influenced your life somehow, or aspire to be like. Put these vision boards in a place that you cannot miss and focus on them daily.

Step 4: Draft your vision statement: Begin to write out your vision clearly stating what you want now and in the future and clearly showing you how you shall achieve it. Keep the vision relatively S.M.A.R.T.E.R (Specific, Measurable, Achievable,

Relevant, Time-bound, Environment-friendly, and Risks-identified). Also decide whether this is an intermediate-term or long-term vision statement.

Step 5: Read your vision first thing in the morning and last thing at night and aim to remember it. Every time you read it, feel your belief in it and say it with meaning. Some days you'll be better at this than others, but don't give up!

Step 6: If someone asks you "what do you want in life" tell them your vision. Any opportunity to share it, you must. This is how your vision becomes part of you. It creates accountability and identity.

Step 7: Network and build relationships with people who specifically share or have a similar vision. Exchange ideas, this will make you smile knowing you have like-minded people around you. A coach or mentor may also be of good use to keep you on track with your vision.

Step 8: Create a mastermind group that aims to be the force that aids you towards, realising your dream. It must contain people who take it seriously and are there to help you, as it is within their own interest (do not just pick anyone for a mastermind group, be picky, they must be interested too).

Follow these steps above and you will have a powerful vision, backed by the right energy!

CHAPTER FOURTEEN

TAKING ACTION

BRIDGE THE CONNECTION BETWEEN ACTION AND RESULTS

The great aim of education is not knowledge but action.

Herbert Spencer

ACTIONS PRODUCE RESULTS

Tony Robbins is one of the world's most renowned thought leaders, focusing much of his life's work on human behaviour and strategy, i.e. determining how one can truly position themselves for success. He states in his model *The Success Cycle* that our human potential determines the level of action we take, your actions determine results, and those results embed a belief that feeds back into your potential. The more certain you are about your ability to achieve, the more aligned you will be to realising your dreams. The dynamics of this cycle must be realised, where it can then be used to produce bigger and high-impacting results. If you analyse *The Success Cycle* you will realise that each stage of the cycle is as important as each other, however action supercharges all factors within the cycle.

Taking action is so important, but people don't take enough of it. Why? Need I say, think about it for yourself, when have you not taken action and what was your reason for it? No one ever really talks about the quality of action you should take, they usually say "take action" and there's a bias towards it. I would suggest we take direction-focused active-action towards our goals. This describes that you are moving towards a point in your life where your attention is on this point, and that you are doing things frequently and deliberately towards reaching that point. Be the person who jumps off a cliff and learns to fly 10 seconds from the ground.

THE MORE ACTION YOU TAKE THE MORE RESULTS YOU CAN PLAY WITH

As aforementioned, the law of averages states that if you do something many times, you're bound to get a desired result, right? Have you ever really tested that theory to see if it's true? When people attempt the law of averages they either never repeat the theory into practice, or, they repeat the theory into practice by doing just a little bit more and then they stop. Look at what is being said "it is a law of averages", in other words you must apply the correct rules using particular procedures and behaviours that elicit a result over multiple attempts; these attempts are to be made until successful. Whilst you have a second quickly look at the definition of "action".

Now that you've taken action on looking for the definition of "action" (if you haven't your satisfying my prior points, go and do it now), it should serve as a reminder of what one does when they act, getting you closer to that definition the more frequently you act. People take action because of three things:

1. A deep need to change their situation.

2. Certainty of what they want.

3. A persistent effort to change habits into permanent success habits.

Look at the list above and see if any of these apply to you. If they do not, then think about why they don't. As said before and I'll say it again, the best way to assess your situation is to ask questions and better yet to take action on them too!

TAKE MASS IMPERFECT ACTION

Do people still want to be perfect in this day and age? It is such a prehistoric mindset to have. To be fair there has been a huge influence from audio and visuals that feed this into our mindset and we have taken it as a *de facto* reality. What is perfect? What you can see, feel, touch, smell, think, sense is as perfect as it's going to get. We aren't in the realm of idealised visuals, mathematical distributions, and evenly-constructed perfection, even though we try to identify with it, we are in the realm of creation, taking action, and learning. There is no opportunity in perfection because essentially everything is done, everything would be complete and in fact it would be quite boring. So, the aim is to take **MASS IMPERFECT ACTION!**

The first time I heard of "mass imperfection action" it immediately clicked, why not open the door for yourself, remove all forms of retreat and sort it out when it comes to it, at least it is done. Yes, I do agree you shouldn't compromise quality too much, on the contrary getting it done is more important because it broadens your horizons and possibilities, you can foresee and identify problems earlier and therefore, take further action. Apply it to your life and see what happens to you, just in 7 days. I am not promising absolute success, but I am suggesting a change in perspective and a feeling towards wanting and doing more.

CHAPTER FIFTEEN

PERSISTENCE

STOPPING IS A WASTE OF TIME AND ENERGY

Let me tell you the secret that has led to my goal. My strength lies solely in my tenacity.

Louis Pasteur

DO NOT SLOW DOWN THE REALISATION OF DREAMS

I love to use food as an example to explain how we respond when we have been dreaming about a meal for a long time. As explained before, you will do anything to satisfy your hunger. I want you to place this imagery in your head again. Let's say you wanted an English breakfast randomly and out of the blue. For lunch, you go on a mission to hunt for a restaurant that will still be serving this full English, but you have to be quick because you realised they stop serving this food in 45 mins. You get to the counter, you're about to pay for it, and then decide "I don't want to waste money and it's too tight for time". You tell the sales assistant not to bother with the order and you walk off back to work.

Your emotional state went from a satisfied, almost orgasmic state, to an extremely frustrated and genuinely heartbroken state. How depressing, if you followed through you would have been smiling for the rest of the day, but you're not. This is your life. When you decide to stop working on your tasks, goals and dreams you not only damage your psychology, you also damage the creation process which shifts to another universal conscious being that will take action. Don't be a fool and stop right before you get gold.

STOPPING CREATES CONFUSION

We have all put ourselves in situations where we have started something with energy and enthusiasm and then over time that feeling of "I'm going to go all out!" fades away like the leaves on an aged tree. After the point of freedom, you begin to focus in on yourself and question, "what is it that I want?" or "why are things not working out?" or "I wasted so much time". With regards to the latter you are right; you did waste time because you gave up.

Giving up confuses people because you go from a state of feeling like you know what you want, to a state of not knowing anymore. It's like following a Google Maps on your smartphone to a destination and then saying you don't want to go there anymore because the journey is tiring and annoying. You put your smartphone and your hands in your pocket and walk around like a lost sheep looking for somewhere to hang. Confusion instils fear and increases anxiety, which cascades into a life that is not fulfilling. Avoid confusion like the plague and stay on track. Do whatever is necessary to stay in the know, understand and take action on it.

On the contrary, sometimes it is ok to stop and do something else, as overtime you have realised it conflicts with your aligned and higher values. This usually happens when a person is not ready for a goal, or has compromised their values for an idealised goal that is not genuine. Your decision making at the beginning is crucial, so give yourself enough time to decide whether it is right to embark on an endeavour.

LEARN TO REST NOT TO STOP

Infants love to stack building blocks on top of each other to create a tower. Sooner or later the tower will fall and they'll have to start again, if you watch them closely they never get defeated at starting the tower again, their aim is to build the tower as high as possible to a point where they are satisfied... which is transient. The aim after that is to keep it up, or ironically knock it down with excited force! The hidden gem here is to have the mentality of a child, don't stop, and keep on moving.

The infant's mindset is very simple in the sense that they stereotypically have a lower frequency of experiences that heavily influence their behaviour. We undoubtedly have had experiences that polarise our perceptions, opinions, ideas and thoughts in a way that alters our action in life, and this can be why we stop projects and plans because of what our mind tells us. How do you know something works if you haven't followed it through, regardless of whether you had to start again? You don't, because you have never hit your goal. That is going to change!

Starting again is part of the process and it gives you thick skin, savviness, and if used correctly, confidence, because you now know a version of how you shouldn't do something. That knowledge is priceless. Metaphorically speaking, **Not everything good starts in heaven, sometimes it starts in hell**.

Learn to understand that the word failure is not really used appropriately in our circles of life, and it could be a deploy word to create confusion and complexity for people. Yes, there are times where you will feel like you haven't achieved enough, but the reverse should always be a learning experience and an understanding that you endured a challenge. See it as a challenge, one where you must see yourself as superior, competing against you and the world. Compare the definitions of "failure" and "challenge" and really think about what they mean.

In order to close this first book of the *Understand, Reach Expand* series, I would like to say focus on these words that a very dear person continuously says to me:

"Believe and Succeed"

…nothing less, nothing else and nothing more.

A PERSONAL NOTE

I assume that by reading this book you are committed to achieving more in life. As you can see, the teachings in this book are not necessarily ground breaking or revolutionary; rather they are things that work when the right established attitudes have been employed in your mind's framework. I truly do believe that if you are determined enough to change your life positively and progressively towards your desired goals, then you will achieve heights that may even surpass your original vision. A result is a validation point for the brain, and emphasises and encourages the fact that more is possible; so aim to get them!

As constructive, positive and helpful ambassadors to each other, if you found the information within this book to be useful, I would very much be grateful if you post a short review on Amazon. Your message and support will really make a huge difference for helping others to decide to take action and for using constructive feedback to make this book even better for future readers.

If you'd like to leave a review, then all you need to do is go to Amazon and search for *Understand Reach Expand: 15 Super Effective Ways to Manage your Mind* and leave a review under the **Customer reviews** section and click on the button **Write a customer review**.

Thanks again for your support!

ABOUT THE AUTHOR

MICHAEL TABIRADE is an enthusiastic and pragmatic achievement coach and personal empowerment educator. He focuses on strategic positioning and behaviour change to adopt a positive impact. Based in London and growing up as a millennial, Michael has been able to learn and manifest these techniques into the NHS, having a proven track record for improving people, teams and services. Connect with Michael via the following social media platforms:

Fb – Michael Tabirade – Achieve More Success
Tw - @Mike_Tabirade
In - @Mike_Tabirade

Learn more about Michael and what he does at
http://michaeltabirade.com

THE 15 MIND MANAGEMENT VALUES

1. *Master your mind*
2. *Build your self-esteem*
3. *Develop your self-image*
4. *Improve your self-awareness*
5. *Evaluate your experiences*
6. *Overcome your fears*
7. *Educate yourself about society*
8. *Determine your required mindset*
9. *Commit to positive change*
10. *Position your willpower for success*
11. *Drive clarity of purpose in everything you do*
12. *Utilise your creativity to manifest your reality*
13. *Strategically influence your behaviour*
14. *Remember, action gives you data*
15. *Never give up, **never stop***